COMMON MISTAKES

at UPSC Civil Services Examination & how to avoid them

Ideas to avoid mistakes at most difficult and misunderstood examination of the world

Abhishek Dular, IPS

HAR-ANAND
PUBLICATIONS PVT LTD

"there's nothing wrong in making mistakes, what's wrong is letting it stay as a mistake without the effort of making it right."

– Anonymous

HAR-ANAND PUBLICATIONS PVT LTD
E-49/3, Okhla Industrial Area, Phase-II, New Delhi-110020
Tel.: 41603490
E-mail: info@haranandbooks.com/haranand@rediffmail.com
Shop online at: www.haranandbooks.com
Like us on www.facebook.com/haranandbooks

Reprint, 2017

Published by Ashok Gosain and Ashish Gosain for Har-Anand Publications Pvt Ltd

Printed in India at Arya Printers.

Introduction

"The only man who never makes mistakes is the man who never does anything."

– Theodore Roosevelt

When I first attempted the exam I always used to think "who else is going to be selected if I am not." The thought of failure never came to my mind. I soon realized that I made the mistake of underestimating level of the exam. One failure at getting shortlisted for interview was followed by another. To my utmost surprise the score in the second attempt at mains was lower than the first attempt.

I always wanted to be a cop. And while I was checking my roll number in the list of candidates called for interview at notice board of UPSC in my second attempt, I saw a Police Gypsy, with two policemen, parked outside the door. That uniform and that police car suddenly appeared beyond my dreams. I don't think I will ever forget that extreme feeling of helplessness. Craving for uniform aggravated to burning desire. I was shattered and it took me some time to get back to normal. The question—"What more can I do?" bothered me for days.

After turning normal in a few days I realized that *it was not just about "what" to prepare. It was more about "how" to prepare. And even much more than that, "why" to prepare.* I started thinking about my mistakes. I started discussing them with my brother and friends. I really thought hard about it. And soon I had a big list of mistakes. I started working on them. I had nothing more to study after two attempts. So I spent most of the time in correcting them.

Years are more precious when we are young. Some mistakes are better managed before they occur. When the stakes are high it is better to learn from the mistakes of others. When I see in retrospect and try to find out why I failed in first two attempts at UPSC Civil services examinations, I find a lot of my shortcomings.

There is no school which teaches the strategy to succeed in the exam except the scattered coaching classes mostly in capital city whose main concern most of the time is enrollment. *Success teaches us much less than the failures.* Whatever I happen to write, I feel, are my own learning during preparation. I sincerely hope that this will bring value to your preparation for civil services examination. While we prepare for this exam we travel towards our goal where we have to make our own way. These mistakes will help you to find your own way. Though it is hard to learn from mistakes of others, but it is difficult to afford otherwise with limited time at our hand.

While some mistakes are committed before the start of the preparation, some are committed during the preparation. Some are committed during the examination and some in between the examination stages. While in some mistakes we get chance to discover, many others are never revealed to us. Some mistakes are out of misunderstandings and some from miscalculations. Some may prove to be minor omission while others could be blunders. Some are learnt by own experiences and some out of other's experiences.

Some of the mistakes are committed because of inaction on known dangers; most of them are committed due to ignorance. Some errors are mistake of facts others are fallacies of attitudes. Some are faults of strategy and planning and some of execution. But all of them revolve around "How", "What" and "Why" of examination.

Cops are busy people. They have n number of jobs to do. But never too busy that they cannot write. Writing improves. Experiences and research are to be shared and discussed rather than just to be clogged in brain. To build a community where aspirants are confident and asset to their family. To make the struggle of Civil Services Aspirants focused and fruitful. To build and cultivate the future leaders of India. To inspire and guide to serve. To develop the capacity to think outside the box and the book. I make an attempt to do all this by writing this book. And so it just happened that I wrote it. It is easy to read and understand. It is short to finish in one go. A book to share and discuss, but only if you like. The book is not just based on my experiences but also my research on the topic. I experienced the contents, brainstormed them and read and discussed about them.

The book has been divided into three parts—Mistakes of Attitude, Mistakes of Preparation Strategies, Mistakes of Exam Strategies.

Contents

PART I: MISTAKES OF ATTITUDE

PART II: MISTAKES OF PREPARATION STRATEGIES

PART III: MISTAKES OF EXAM STRATEGIES

PART I
Mistakes of Attitude

Chapter 1
Delay in Deciding

"Delay always breeds danger;
and to protract a great
design is often to ruin it."

– Miguel de Cervantes

Civil services is a job where getting early is equally important as getting into. The promotions are generally time bond and therefore getting early will give you the age benefit. You will be more probable to reach to the top in the particular civil service for which you are selected.

You will have more chances of leading your organization. You will have more time to serve and therefore the probability of making a big difference will increase. You shall have enough time to prepare if you decide and start early. You will have flexibility in deciding the next attempt if you don't make it in one attempt.

With age we become more hardened in attitudes. In the preparation we need to change our attitude also. The aggression and risk taking ability declines with age and so declines the ability to slog and take on the setbacks. The power to get trained and assimilate reduces. At younger age you have lower social commitments. Your parents can help you and will not have much expectation from you financially and socially. You will not have friends who already started earning.

You need a certain amount of time for your apprenticeship. Starting early will also reduce your competition. Even if you do not make it in the end you can go for further studies and alternate job at a decent age. All these advantages will certainly increase your confidence of taking the exam and cracking it.

CHAPTER 2

Know the Purpose

"He who has a why to live for
can bear almost any how."

– Friedrich Nietzsche

Why do you want to get into civil services? Why are you preparing for the exam? The answer is the purpose of taking the exam. All the effort and hard work is incomplete without the purpose. The purpose will give you amazing energy and power to keep going.

Think about it. It could be to become a leader, having power to effect and improve lives of others through vision, hard work, creativity, determination, courage and commitment. To be financially free, to earn name and place in society, to be a living example of what a human can do, to fulfill a dream. To be confident, energetic, enthusiastic, independent and self-sufficient person. To stretch my limits, to motivate others and to realize my full potential as a human. To be courageous, fearless and one who is always in habit of thinking big and going the extra mile. To be a role model. To create a legacy.

Once you know the purpose, write it down. You can keep on reading this written purpose. May be daily or in a few days.

This will entirely change your attitude towards the exam. Merely reading it will give you power. Get connected with your purpose. You got to live your own purpose and nobody else's. Create a meaning for your decision.

It will give you focus and you will not question your own decision even when you are feeling down and out due to failure. It will give you a direction and sense of fulfillment and keep on supplying you unlimited drive towards your goal. You will be able to give your 100% and will not deviate towards the things that do not matter.

So take charge of your life and have your purpose. Don't delay it. Write it down today. And if you have doubts about taking the exam, better leave it. You can have no commitment with doubts.

Chapter 3
Estimate the Competition

"If you are insecure, guess what?
The rest of the world is too.
Do not overestimate the competition
and underestimate yourself.
You are better than you think."

– T. Harv Eker

The exam has three different stages—Prelims, mains and personality test. The first stage is an elimination round. The number of candidates admitted in the mains exam is around 12-13 times the number of vacancies. Number of candidates selected for personality test is around two times the number of vacancies.

The exam is no doubt one of the toughest examinations of world. The selection rate is around 0.2%. But this is when we calculate it on the basis of number of candidates who fill the prelims form to the finally selected. In fact, generally only 50% of the candidates, who fill the form, appear for prelims. Even many of those who appear in the prelims do not have this goal of getting into civil services as their most important goal. So, the competition is largely at the level of mains and the personality test.

Competition at the examination is thus mostly overestimated. That is why the decision to prepare is taken with awe. A rare few also underestimate the exam. In either case one should be aware of the true level of competition. This is essential in taking the decision of going for the exam. Don't run away from it because of overestimation or underestimation. The reputation of exam in our society will mostly push you towards overestimation about level of competition. Like most of the things it is not what it seems from outside.

So, don't get frightened and submit to fear.

CHAPTER 4

Decided. Go for It!

"Waste no more time arguing about what a good man should be. Be one."

– Marcus Aurelius

Once you have decided to take the exam there is no point in wasting the time in preparing for the preparation. Some aspirants feel that they need to study a lot general nature books before they are ready to start the preparation. They feel that even for taking a coaching they need to coach themselves. Therefore they start reading a lot of books outside the syllabus. They also accumulate a lot of such books.

It prolongs our preparation time and we lose focus. Our energy gets diverted and the output is not proportional to the effort. Preparation is more like a one day cricket more than a test match. We need to save our wicket and score also.

So stop this procrastination. Once you have decided to take the plunge then go for it. Don't take time in getting comfortable before the preparation. *You need not prepare for the preparation.*

CHAPTER 5

Ban the Broadcast

Zip The Lip Theory:
If you've got something
good going, keep it quiet.

– Robert Ringer

UPSC civil services exam is one of the toughest competitions of India. In fact it is difficult to find such a difficult and long drawn process of selection for any other job across the globe. The mere thought of deciding to prepare for it invites awe. The civil services are still one of the most prestigious jobs of India. Apart from the hard and smart work, intelligence and many more qualities, you require luck. You are never sure when you will finally make it.

Telling the people around us about our goal of clearing this exam invites sarcastic remarks and ridicule. Except your most dear ones do not share this idea with anybody. You will put yourself in unnecessary pressure by telling the world about it. People might scare you about the exam rather than appreciating. You will get to listen more failure stories than success stories. People will talk of alternate career options. Some will question the relevance of the exam. Some will question the integrity of UPSC. Some will question your competence sarcastically. *So don't present your goals but present their accomplishment to the world. Goals are better written than spoken.*

If ever you want to discuss about it with your friends, acquaintances and family members do it before you decide to take the exam. Once you have decided to take the exam never disclose your one of the toughest goal. In fact, it is true for any other important goals you have in life. People will end up discouraging you. Until you have completed the goal keep it to yourself. Dangers of telling to others are many unless you trust the other person completely. So work in silence about your goal of making it to the civil services.

And God help those who try to impress others by saying that they are preparing for civil services.

CHAPTER 6
Don't Bother What They Say

"I have often wondered how it is
that every man loves himself more
than all the rest of men, but yet sets
less value on his own opinions of
himself than on the opinions of others."

– Marcus Aurelius

Let us not worry about what people say. My grandfather once told me story in my childhood. It goes like this. Once upon a time a grandfather and grandson were moving on a path to their village with a horse. Grandfather was sitting on the horse and the grandson was walking besides. Looking at them a person coming from other side said "how unfair, the man is sitting on horse and the little kid is walking." Giving value to what the person said, they changed positions. The grandson then started riding and the grandfather started walking besides till they met another man coming from opposite direction. Looking at them he commented, "how unfair, the old man is walking and the young grandson is sitting on horseback." Again after listening to what he said they acted and both of them now started riding the horse till they again met a person. This time the person said, "how unfair, two people are riding one poor horse." Getting frustrated both of them started walking besides the horse. After sometime they again met a person who looking at them commented, "how unfair, what is the use of keeping a horse when one has to walk on foot." When the person left the grandfather and grandson started deliberations. The grandfather, who was aware about value of all what different people said, explained to his grandson that if one keep on listening to other people and keep on acting one can only be unhappy.

While we may listen to others but we should act independently. We cannot live our life by worrying about the feelings of others.

CHAPTER 7

Give Cent Percent

"We must all suffer
one of two things:
the pain of discipline
or the pain of regret
and disappointment."

– Jim Rohn

The exam requires and deserves your 100% effort. Once you do it the result no longer matters. The exam required 100%. You gave 100%. That's the end of it. It doesn't matter if you are selected or not.

You increase your chances by giving 100%. And you will have no regrets. You will never feel that you could have achieved it, if you fail it. Do not allow the fear and intimidation of the exam to reduce your effort. If you cannot give 100% for one of your most cherished dream, the chances are that you will never give it to any other task in life. This is our most important task and number one priority. And it is only possible if you leave the less important out. Leave the tasks that are not important. *Delegate, drop or defer the unimportant tasks so that you can give your 100%.*

Some aspirants try to pursue a degree along with preparation. Some take a fulltime or part time job. Some pursue relationships and friendships. Some are in love affairs. Some get caught in social obligations. This is a dangerous venture. Don't hesitate to take help of your parents for your finances. If that is not possible take a loan. Don't waste time in earning livelihood simultaneously with preparation.

CHAPTER 8
Waiting is Wasting

There are only two mistakes
one can make along the road
to truth; not going all the way,
and not starting.

– Buddha

The exam has three different stages—prelims, mains and interview. There is a time gap between every stage exam and the result of that stage. Most of such time is wasted in waiting for the result. We do not put our heart and soul in preparation till the result is out at every stage. This is because of uncertainty of clearing that stage. They feel that it is only when they qualify for a particular level that they will start preparing seriously for it. This mistake costs you time and an attempt.

After taking prelims don't wait for result. Calculate your score based on answers provided by some reputed coaching. These days there are also many websites which provide answers. Based on these suggested answers you can have a reasonable estimate of your chances of clearing the prelims. Every year UPSC also declares the cut-off marks of previous years. You can take that cut-off as standard measure and calibrate it according to the number of seats. The level of exam hardly changes in a year. So there is no point in estimating based on the difficulty of the prelims unless there is a big change. This will clear the uncertainty. There are three things possible here—first, your score is high and you will clear it. Second, your score is on the border line and you may or may not make it. In both these situations start preparing for the mains immediately. The third situation is that you are going to miss it with a margin. In this case also start preparing for the mains. This is because you don't need much time in preparing for the prelims. The next prelim exam is anyway far. So, start preparing for the mains from the day one and never wait for the result of prelims. The worst case is that you will not be selected in prelims. Even then you shall have the chance of taking the exam again.

Again after taking the mains don't wait for it result. After a small break start preparing for the next mains exam. This is because this time will never come back again. If you do not clear mains and want to take one more attempt, the preparation done during this period will help a lot. This is also because you don't need too much time to prepare for the personality test. You can do it even after the result of mains.

Furthermore, after taking the interview don't wait for the result. Start preparing for the next mains. You must never forget that prelim exam is only a screening test. Its marks are not going to count.

The most important exam is the mains because it is where the marks will count. So get your preparation focus on mains and stop waiting for the results.

Chapter 9
Suffering the Pressure

"Pressure is something you feel
when you don't know what the
hell you're doing."

– Peyton Manning,
American football player

Getting into Civil Services is a difficult career choice. When we prepare for it we are in early 20s. That's the time we are supposed to be doing something and earning. You will have your social and family commitments in this age. You will at least need the financial support of your family if not any other support. You cannot do a job and simultaneously prepare for the exam. Pressure in such circumstances is inevitable. But to suffer or not to suffer is in your hand. It is better to feel the pressure and manage it rather than ignoring it or yielding to it.

Pressure could be because of expectations of the family, friends and teachers. Because of the perceived failure and the difficulty of exam. Pressure of studying the entire syllabus in a limited time. There could be more reasons also.

There are ways to handle the pressure. Having a purpose for getting into civil services is the foremost. You must set our study goals and achieve them one by one. You must make schedule of your studies. You must stay away from the negative people and the avoid distractions. You need enough sleeps and breaks during our preparation. *Much of the fear can be eliminated through good preparation and exposing yourself to the exam atmosphere through the mock tests regularly.* Organizing your study material, notes and written answers will also help. Relaxing physical exercises and meditation will also assist.

And most important of all is the belief that we can live with pressure and yet do not suffer it.

CHAPTER 10

Faith

"The question isn't who is
going to let me;
it's who is going to stop me."

– Ayn Rand

Criticizing the exam, once you have decided to prepare is counter-productive. Whatever be the quality and style of exam and the conducting organization, it is you who decided to go for the exam at the first place. Union Public Service Commission is one unsung hero of India. It has been serving the nation for so many years now. It is one of the foremost agencies in Nation building.

Stay away from people who criticize the exam or the agency. It is one of the toughest tasks to select the best candidates from a huge variety of background, culture, region and language. Don't blame the commission or the exam pattern for your failures. Take the responsibility for yourself. The commission and the pattern of exam are same for everybody. *The same wind is blowing for everybody. It is only how you set our sails. You cannot change the direction of the wind. You can only adjust your sails.*

If you face an unsuccessful attempt try to find out the mistakes that you committed. Never try to find the mistakes of the Commission or coaching, the exam pattern, study material or the system in general. You are responsible for all your choices and mistakes. And you can correct them if you want. You can hardly correct the system or faults in things beyond you. You have no control over the outside factors.

So, have faith in the exam, the commission and yourself. You want to do it and you are willing to do it. That's the end of it.

CHAPTER 11
Prepare and Play

"Victorious warriors win first and then go to war, while defeated warriors go to war first and then seek to win"

– Sun Tzu, The Art of War

Every aspirant need to know the number of attempts he or she is ready to take for the examination. It largely depends upon your age, your resolve, family and financial support, the scope of improvement, ability to find and correct mistakes in previous attempts and your level of preparation.

Most of our mistakes and shortcomings are disclosed after taking an attempt. But this can also be done and felt by taking a lot of mock test before the examination. Taking mock tests is nothing but taking the attempts without being counted. You can minimize your attempts this way.

Plan for a single attempt only or at the maximum two attempts. And take this attempt seriously and with full preparation. A failed attempt without preparation is not just waste of attempt but also a toll on your confidence and resolve.

So prepare with a plan and take exam only when you are prepared.

Chapter 12

Main is Mains

"Obstacles are those frightful
Things you see when you take
your eyes off your goal."

– Henry Ford

Aspirants fear the prelims a lot more than it deserve. Calculate the ratio of seats with prelims selected candidates. The marks are not going to be counted for the final selection. It is only screening exam. We need not be in the top 100 to succeed. You just need to be better than the cutoff. You don't need to put in everything. The value in terms of time is not commensurate with the effort. The result is that we spend a lot of time in preparing for the prelims.

We go for all kinds of books available in the market and try to read them and memorize them. There is nothing wrong in reading books. But the selection of books is not focused. We tend to overdo the study part. In fact at the prelims stage we need more of practice of solving the objective questions than just reading books.

Moreover while preparing for the mains a lot of topics mentioned in prelims syllabus are automatically covered. Overemphasis on prelim exam happens because of lack of confidence. This in turn is because of the fact that only a few percent of aspirants take the previous year question papers and solve them like mock test and see their performance. Once you know your performance in few such tests you will become more comfortable in assessing the situation and your chances. Also you need to know the probable previous year cutoff so that you can have realistic estimate of your standing. *If you are not so far from the cutoff then forget about reading books for the prelims.* You can then just practice a lot of objective questions available from various sources. Focus on the mains in such a situation. Even if you are in the range of 70% of the cutoff you can still cover it through practice tests and mains preparation.

In the world athletics competitions and in the Olympics we have heats for the participants for selecting them for final competition. Participants who know where they stand do not sweat it out in the heats. In fact in heats of 100m anybody hardly clocks less than 10 seconds and during the finals anybody hardly crosses 10 seconds.

So don't take your eyes off the mains and don't overemphasis and burn it out in prelim exam.

CHAPTER 13

Opting for Optional

"We are our choices."

– Jean-Paul Sartre

Choice of optional is a crucial decision. Some aspirants try an optional and then change it after an unsuccessful attempt. This is like starting the race again.

The choice of optional depends upon the availability of study material, your interest and confidence in the subject, scoring pattern of the subject, guidance, your subject in graduation/post graduation, and coaching available. Take your time in deciding the optional and do not rush for it. Previous years question papers can help and so will the syllabus of a particular optional. Discuss it with your friends, parents and others. You don't need to be conservative here. Many professionals like engineers and doctors don't choose their own optional but go for social sciences subjects. Such people have topped the exam also.

And once you have taken a thoughtful decision, stick to it. In the middle of preparation and after taking an unsuccessful attempt don't go for change in optional. Ultimately it is you and your preparation that makes the optional successful rather than optional making you successful.

CHAPTER 14
Mentors

"Tell me and I forget,
teach me and I may remember,
involve me and I learn."

– Benjamin Franklin

Mentor is somebody who gives us advice. A person who is experienced and who can guide the less experienced. One who inspires and motivates us. One who can tell you about your strengths and weaknesses.

In the pursuit of civil services examination we need a mentor to guide us. It is impossible to learn everything from the books. It could be one or more. We need experienced and successful candidates whom we can talk and discuss about preparation. Mentoring will give us edge and we will have someone to look upon to for support and guidance. Don't be alone in your struggle. Have someone to guide you and to look upon to.

Your coaches, parents and friends could also be your mentors for specific issues. Expect nobody to tell you who can be a good mentor. Try to find out your own mentor. Someone in the civil services. Or maybe your coaches. You can meet him periodically or at least talk on phone. And let us not make ourselves small by feeling "I am not that good, who will be my mentor." Try to find and you will get him or her.

Two often neglected mentors are your Mom and Dad.

CHAPTER 15

What Went Wrong?

"The man who never alters
his opinions is like standing water,
and breeds reptiles of the mind"

– William Blake

Often an unsuccessful attempt is followed by another mistake. This is the mistake of not identifying the reasons for "What went wrong?" Questions like—what can I do better? What could be the possible mistakes I committed? What are the known knowns and unknown knowns? In simple words it is about finding the mistakes that you committed and a strategy to correct them.

We just think that we were not well prepared. We feel that we just need to study more and more. Attend more coaching. Study more books. This is a mistake.

We need to ponder the reasons for not being successful. You can analyze your performance based on your score. Devote time and think about it. Otherwise the chances are that you will not realize your mistakes and will repeat them. *The exam is all about identifying and learning from your mistakes.* We are the one who can do best in identifying mistakes committed by us. After identifying reasons we need to work on them. Plan your strategy to correct your particular mistake. Different mistakes may require different strategies to correct them.

And of course, the mistakes discussed here will help you to find your own.

CHAPTER 16

I Won't Give Up

I hated every minute of training, but I said, "Don't quit. Suffer now and live the rest of your life as a champion."

– Muhammad Ali

More than anything else the exam requires a resolve. The ability to motivate ourselves and to keep going even after failures. It is easy to give up in such a competitive examination. But the exam is worth trying and giving your 100%. It could very well be your toughest challenge in life. There is beauty in pursuing such a tough goal like this. Even if you finally do not make it, for whatever reasons, you come of it as a better man. A more evolved man. *Most of the traits required to be a successful civil servant are gained during the preparation itself.* Let the surrender be graceful if it has to be surrender finally. The one which we do not regret. When you think of giving up think of the reason why you held on so long.

Don't confuse here between giving up and having enough of it. The two are entirely different. Letting go doesn't mean giving up, but accepting that it cannot be done. I know it is easy to give up just after the news of unsuccessful attempt. That is a difficult time. But hold on. That time will pass. When you decide to take again or leave it, take your time. Don't rush to any conclusion. It is a crucial life decision. Don't underestimate yourself. What you are capable of? You are more than what you think you are capable of. You can find a different strategy of achieving your goal if you fail in one. Still another, even if you fail again. Let the good work you have done preparing be not lost for a little more work and effort.

CHAPTER 17

A Backup Plan

"Tomorrow is not another day;
tomorrow is today's backup plan."

– Ian Coburn

Having a backup career plan will always give you more confidence. This is true for most of the aspirants except the real daredevils who derive their energy and motivation by virtue of having no backup plan.

As the success percentage is very low most of us have this fear "what if I am not selected finally." This fear is better managed than ignored. Those having a backup plan will not be guided by this fear.

You could do a professional degree course during your graduation or post graduation. You could appear for other exams conducted by UPSC for different job. State PSC is also an option. You could go for short term professional courses to secure a job. There are n number of ways to secure a good job. May be, plan to be an entrepreneur.

Transition to backup plan has to be timed properly. Devote time to it only when you are done with your plan.

And if you can justify not having a backup plan, have your reasons. Know why you don't want any backup plan.

CHAPTER 18

Break the Shield

"The journey is the reward."

– Chinese Proverb

Most of us try to build an armor of knowledge by reading a number of books over a long period of time during preparation. We wait for the armor to get stronger and stronger. We want it to be impenetrable. The quest to get failure-proof is never ending. One can never be completely ready this way. The only alternative is to expose oneself to danger. To hurt oneself. Comfort can be achieved only by getting out of comfort. Make yourself uncomfortable. You need not love your preparation. But you know what it can make you. So get used to small fights through mock tests. You will get hurt. It is good to get hurt before the examination. Get hurt from your performance in mock test in every possible way. This way you are only improving yourself. When you get hurt you won't repeat mistakes. And you will commit newer mistakes. Soon you will reach a level where you have identified most of your shortcomings.

The best part of having a big goal is that, even if one does not achieve it, the person one becomes while achieving the goal. Even if someone takes away our goal from us after achieving, what we became in achieving the goal cannot be taken away from us by anyone. The preparation in itself is the training to become a good civil servant. The journey will give you improved willpower, better discipline, more skills and ultimately more confidence. The long hours of preparation, the risk with time, energy and money will change you to be a better human being. You will break all the limits that you once fixed for yourself. You will thus set even higher goals for yourself in future. These changes in Self will help us in achieving future goals.

PART II

Mistakes of Preparation Strategies

CHAPTER 1

Study Plan

"If you don't design your own life plan, chances are you'll fall into someone else's plan. And guess what they have planned for you? Not much."

– Jim Rohn

Study plan is all about devoting your preparation time to various subjects. It is schedule of your study goals. All the papers of the exam are important. It is about how you plan your day; week; month and year during preparation. It is about setting goals for you with deadlines and quantitative outputs. How you are going to cover the various topics of the syllabus. How you will devote time for studies; for notes making; for answer writing; for mock exams etc. How you are going to revise. In short, it is answer to the "How" and "What" of the preparation. What you are going to do and how you are going to do it.

A plan will give you confidence and will take away the exam pressure. You manage your time well and slowly inch towards success every day. Success at exam is sum of all the successes you experience every day. Plan will make you visualize your dream. It will assist in concentrating better and retain the syllabus. And you will not miss out the important topics. The plan will make you more accountable to yourself.

But don't be overambitious here. Make it realistic and achievable by you. Don't make a study plan of 18 hours in a day. It should not be more than 10-12 hours. Depending upon your performance in executing the plan you may change it periodically. Making a study plan and not executing it is even more demoralizing than not having a plan.

A study plan is like breaking a big goal into many small goals to be achieved every day. Nothing can be executed without a plan.

Chapter 2

Important First

"Things which matter most
must never be at the mercy
of things which matter least."

– Johann Wolfgang von Goethe

While making a study plan we try to cover each and every topic of the syllabus with equal focus. We can very well narrow down our focus to more important topics first. Our time should be utilized first for the most important things especially when we are short of time. Focus can be attained through analysis of previous year question papers. Moreover based on the choice given to answer the questions we can narrow down our focus.

This can be practiced in our first attempt if we are short of time. Of course, we should try to cover everything if we have enough time. Moreover don't neglect your weak topics.

The underlying idea is to have focus by separating the important topics from the ordinary. It will make your preparation more productive. *Doing the more important topics first must be the agenda then.* Doing the more important first will give you confidence and sets the momentum.

CHAPTER 3

Short Study Group

"Keep away from people who
try to belittle your ambitions.
Small people always do that,
but the really great make you
feel that you, too, can become great."

– Mark Twain

Study group is a group of students who regularly meet and interact about their common study field. For civil services exam a group of 2 to 4 persons is good enough. Study group has a lot of advantages for all it members.

Study group helps us to develop a sense of competition. It helps us in making study plan and executing it. Group members discuss study topics, inspire and motivate each other. It assists us in identifying our strengths and weaknesses. When one person explains a concept to others it reinforces in his mind. Problems and solutions are discussed and solved together. It lends a helping hand in evaluating answers written on probable questions. It reveals your level of preparation. You learn from each other's mistakes. It is both an intellectual and emotional support.

You speak out loud in front of your group and it helps in internalizing the topics learnt. You can share books, notes and study material. You can brainstorm together and prepare your list of probable questions from the syllabus. It makes the study more enjoyable and gives you a break from monotonous study alone. *You are less likely to delay the execution of your study plan.* You will develop critical thinking skills and thinking from different perspectives. It will improve your confidence and reduces the exam pressure. You can ask questions freely which you cannot do in class.

Care has to be taken in identifying the group members. Members must be of similar academic level and committed towards achieving their goals. Gossiping and negative discussions must be avoided.

Chapter 4
Probable Questions

"He who asks a question is a fool
for five minutes; he who does not ask
a question remains a fool forever."

–Chinese proverb

Have your list of probable questions and previous year's questions on every topic of the syllabus. Even before you study and make notes have this list in mind. Your mind works better when the problem or the question is known before the study. It makes your study focused. You start preparing from the point of view of exam rather than simple leisure reading for gaining knowledge.

The probable list of the questions will not be very large, on a topic, even if you include all types of possible questions. You can take help of coaching in refining your list. Keep it dynamic by updating it as you gain more and more confidence through your mock tests.

So make an exhaustive list of probable questions on all topics of syllabus. Search for their answers. *Chances are that questions in exam questions will not be very different.*

It is like putting yourself into the shoes of examiner and thinking how will you set the exam.

CHAPTER 5
Necessity of Notes

"If you want a thing done well,
do it yourself."
–Napoleon Bonaparte

Is it okay to keep on studying from various sources without a way of making it sure that you revise it also at regular intervals? With so many books and study material how do you focus on syllabus? How do you reduce the time required for every subsequent revision? How do you author your own study material? How to keep on reducing the total reading material? How to separate the essential from non-essential?

You take care of all these questions by making your own notes. Notes making will be your first revision of the study material. It will make sure that you apply your mind on the topic and make notes about the important points of a particular topic of syllabus. It is an interactive activity with yourself which will also develop your critical thinking ability. Notes making includes both taking notes from lectures and your own notes while studying.

Knowing the previous year's question papers and your own list of probable questions will further assist you to make better notes. You can convert the complex language mentioned in books to simple words. And when you think and write about a topic it gets internalized.

Notes making is great for understanding a topic better. You spend more time with the topic and therefore remember it better. It helps in organizing your thoughts and improves your handwriting and writing speed. It upgrades your presentation skills. *Most of the times information about a topic is scattered at various place in books and other study materials. All this can be brought to one place through notes making.* Your notes are dynamic and you can keep on updating them when you find something new on that topic. Notes help in your group study and discussion.

You can make flowcharts, use bullet points, maps, diagrams, mindmaps and sketches in your notes. You can highlight the links among the sub-topics. This will make revision of the notes easier and faster.

Notes making sounds time consuming. Yet, it is much more efficient and effective way of learning. After all you cannot keep on reading many different books and reading material every time. So, get rid of the books and increase the power of your revision through notes making.

CHAPTER 6
Answer Writing Practice

"We are what we repeatedly do.
Excellence, then, is not an act, but a habit."
– Aristotle

Most of the aspirants devote most of their preparation time in study and notes making. Gaining knowledge through study is good but our aim is to do well in the exam. The exam consists of questions to be answered. Good answers are not just reproduction of knowledge alone. It is about telling the examiner through your presentation that you know the topic, you understand it, you can analyze and evaluate, and you are comfortable writing about it. *Most of us assume that if we study and know the topic well we can write about it. It is not like that.*

Every answer in exam is constrained by time limit. So if you have not practiced writing answers you will not be able to do well during the exams. So when you are finished studying and making notes about a topic prepare a list of probable questions. These questions can be based on previous year's question papers and your reasonable guesses. Your coaching or tutor can also help in identifying probable questions on a particular topic. Prepare this list and start writing answers. You can take help of your study material and notes to make a good answer.

To begin with you can keep time open for answer writing and gradually shrink the time so that exam conditions are simulated. Slowly you will have a long list of good answers. You can get feedback from your study group, coaches and mentors about the quality of the answer. These answers will be of great help in revision just before the examination.

Most of us delay this practice of answer writing. We keep on studying and studying. Sometimes even if we know that answer writing practice is important, we delay it. We think that once we are finished reading the entire syllabus we will start this practice. This is a bad idea. Largely because when we finish studying a topic (an individual part of syllabus) our mind is fresh about the topic. We can think better in terms of probable questions. We can also write better answers when we have studied the topic recently. Our memory is limited and it fades if we do not repeat it after some time. Practicing answer writing will ensure a repeat study as we would be writing answers referring our study material.

Imagine if you cannot write answers with open book and open time, can you write them in exam. Just think about it. A lot of people have the knowledge but only a few have writing and presentation skills.

CHAPTER 7

Measure of Studies

"He who would learn to fly one day
must first learn to stand and walk
and run and climb and dance;
one cannot fly into flying."

–Friedrich Nietzsche

Many aspirants are generally shy of taking mock test. It could be mock test of prelims, mains or interview. While those who gets interview call generally do not ignore them. At other levels it is often underestimated. People keep on studying for years without even practicing mock exams.

There are many reasons why not taking mock tests is a bad idea. Exam is all about doing well in the limited time of exam. How so ever well read you are, doing better in exam is a different ball game altogether. You cannot just feel good by studying alone. The confidence that you need while facing the exam can only be earned by practicing similar exams many times before the exam.

By practicing them you will take real exam as just another mock test. Hence the awe of exam is reduced. You will be able to sleep well night before the examination. The exam day will be just another day in your preparation.

Many of your shortcomings are only disclosed to you when you take exam like mock exams. One mock test is not good enough for that. You need a lot of them on various topics of syllabus. *This way you will get to know about most of your mistakes before the actual exam.* You will have time to work on your mistakes before it is too late. You will take care of these mistakes in future and therefore your further studies, notes making and answer writing will improve with every mock test.

In mock test you get your answer sheet back after evaluation from the examiner. You get chance to see your evaluated answer sheet. It is not possible in the actual exam. You can further evaluate those sheets and find out how you could have improved. You also get a score for your performance. You will get a lot of score cards before the final score card. This score will also help you to know where you stand among other aspirants.

Mock tests will take out the terror of examination. It will help you get out of attitude of waiting for the studies to be over. Mind it, studies will never be over. *It will complete the different levels of preparation which started with study and notes making followed by answer writing practice.* In general it will help you to stop procrastination. And some exam strategies can be only learnt during the mock tests.

The mock tests will save a lot of time utilized for preparing prelims. Once you have reached a level you don't need to prepare again and for prelims through reading books and study material. The mock tests will ensure that you go up from that level.

Not just your knowledge but your time management strategy is also practiced in the mock tests. Decision about the sequence of questions to be answered is perfected before the actual exam. And so is the decision of picking up from choice questions. The mock tests will expose your mind again and again to the stress situation of thinking and writing in time limit.

The experience of finishing study of a topic with mock test is fulfilling and liberating. We can hardly afford to be a sitting duck to be butchered in the examination. Failures in the mock tests are immediately forgotten as we are learning and correcting our mistakes. Failure in the actual exam because of not taking the mock tests is generally shattering. So, wake up and face the mock tests. You will never be fully ready. And make this goal quantitative and with a deadline. That, by so and so date I will take so many mock tests.

And when your parents or dear ones ask you "how is your preparation going?" don't just tell them that you are studying. Tell them the measure of your studies i.e. mock tests.

Chapter 8
Memory

"Remember my friend, that knowledge is stronger than memory, and we should not trust the weaker"

– Bram Stoker, Dracula

Burdening memory with a lot of facts and figures is a common mistake committed by aspirants. Memorizing and cramming only brings a temporary confidence and relief. There are many reasons why memorizing is bad.

Anything on our memory is bound to get forgotten if it is not practiced, repeated and rehearsed. Especially when the syllabus is vast and you need to prepare over a long period of time.

If we have memorized a topic and a question is asked from the same topic, we will tend to write more of what we memorized rather than critical thinking in the exam. Questions will not be straight so that you will be able to write immediately what you memorized on a particular topic. You will overestimate the quality of your answer. Memorizing will inhibit your learning through understanding fundamentals.

We learn and remember by studying, making notes, writing answers, discussing and solving problem. We also remember through committing mistakes in the mock tests and later realizing the mistakes. It is reinforced and internalized though repeatedly doing so. We need to feed our memory again and again. And the most advanced stage is to teach somebody about that topic and you will not forget it. You may do this in your study group.

So let us forget about memorizing. Get the concepts and fundamentals of syllabus assimilated in your memory through repeat cycle of studying, notes making, answer writing, practice tests and discussions.

Chapter 9
Good Coaching

"People seldom improve when they have no other model but themselves to Copy."

– Oliver Goldsmith.

Coaching is one indispensible need. There are many reasons for that.

When you attend coaching you meet a lot of your fellow competitors. You learn and grow with them. During the mock tests you get to know where you stand. *Certain coaches are very charismatic and their company inspires you.* The study group that you need can be selected out of your classmates.

It will make you less likely to deviate from the syllabus and thereby makes you focused. And when you are paying to learn, you take it more seriously. Coaching can bring out the best in you. It makes you achieve your 100%. It allows you to stretch your limits. It increases the productivity of your time. It is limited in time. So you tend to cover the entire syllabus.

You learn about the right books to read. You get good readymade notes which save a lot of time. It sets in a schedule of study for you. The mock tests which are generally ignored are a routine part of coaching. If you study before going to the class about the topic which they are going to cover in the class, it gets etched into your mind when the same thing is taught in the class. And when you repeat it again it gets internalized.

The decision here is to select the right coaching. And the right time. Try to finish your coaching as soon as possible after you decide to take the plunge. Some aspirants take coaching between the times from prelims to mains. This is not the right time. Finish it before the prelims. You may take a short term capsule course just before the mains to cover the current affairs part. You can choose a place close to your coaching institute for staying. This will save time taken in commuting.

Some institutes also provide notes and reading material. But take care in not accumulating unnecessarily reading material. Some people feel that they should have a minimum level of knowledge before they start taking coaching. So they spend lot of time in reading and gaining knowledge before they take coaching. Most of the people overdo it and in this pursuit lose focus from the syllabus. This is not at all required. Start your coaching without delay. Learn as you are coached.

CHAPTER 10

Distractions

"Work is hard.

Distractions are plentiful.

And time is short."

– Adam Hochschild

Having an organized study room and table is what our school used to tell. It is about having a not so untidy study room. Having a good study table and a chair. We will be spending a lot of months or a few years during our preparation in that room. It is our first direct interaction of our mind and body with the outside world. It sets the ambience. The room alone might be serving as study, library, bedroom, dining and drawing room. Most of prefer quiet surrounding for studies. So have a place away from noise.

Though a trivial issue, it is often forgotten. The result is constant and slow distraction which is difficult to notice and correct. Clear your room of all the unnecessary items and junk.

The biggest distraction are the people and more so the negative people. You tend to put yourself into useless conversation and gossiping. With negative people you tend to question the style and integrity of the exam, thereby losing the faith in exam.

Stay away from distractions like phone, TV, emails, computer etc. These distractions eat away your time, energy and momentum. *Preparing with distractions is like running a race uphill with weights tied on your legs. More the distractions, heavier the weights and steeper the slope uphill.*

This world is far away from being perfect. It is full of stumbling blocks and negativities. Our job is to bypass them and move ahead and not get stuck in them. Our time and energy is limited. Other resources like motivation, zeal, positivity are also limited and require careful investment. Let us be like water. Change state depending upon temperature and pressure and speed depending upon altitude. Bypass the impediments and cut the rocks with constant flow.

I will not discuss more than that on this issue it. You know it is important. Take care of it.

CHAPTER 11

High on Health

"To keep the body in good health is a duty ... otherwise we shall not be able to keep our mind strong and clear."

– Buddha

Do you also need physical fitness apart from mental alertness for the exam? Is time devoted to physical exercises a waste while you prepare for exam? The answer is yes and no respectively. Physical health is indispensible to succeed in any walk of life.

Physical exercises for 30 to 60 minutes, three to four times in a week will be sufficient enough. It could be jogging, playing some sport, breathing exercises or stretching exercises. This will help in reducing the exam stress as it is a recreational activity. You will be able to sleep and study better.

Apart from physical exercises you need a good diet. You body is a machine and the food is the fuel. Some are already in the habit of doing physical exercises and having a good diet. Others will have to develop this habit. And everybody knows about it. The need is just to practice it.

CHAPTER 12

Rest Revitalizes

"Finally, from so little sleeping and
so much reading, his brain dried up
and he went completely out of his mind."

– Miguel de Cervantes Saavedra, Don Quixote

Lack of quality sleep is a very common issue among the aspirants. This is based on a misunderstanding that one needs to study for more than 15 hours in day to prepare for the civil services examination.

Not getting enough sleep is a detriment to our ability to learn and retain information. It's essential to get enough sleep and breaks occasionally. If you don't sleep well and take rest you are prone to sleep in classroom and poor concentration. You do not participate in class with your full attention. Insufficient sleep can cause illness and anxiety. Sleep heals your body and improves your judgment and mental clarity.

Not only sleep it is the schedule of sleep every day that is important. You cannot afford to sleep at different time every day. So, similar to study plan make a sleep plan. Set a sleep schedule, and do your best to get to bed and arise at roughly the same time each day. A nap in the afternoon is also very refreshing and increases your efficiency at studying.

You need some physical activity also everyday to keep your mind alert. If you cannot devote time for it compensate it by being active though out your day.

You performance is greatly improved by getting a full night's sleep. If you find yourself falling asleep in class, or you're always fatigued, try to balance your studying with sleep.

CHAPTER 13
Avoid Accumulating the Unnecessary

"Art is the elimination of the unnecessary."

– Pablo Picasso

Read the syllabus and re-read it. We need to get focused on the requirement only. There is an overwhelming tendency to accumulate a lot of books. There is no need to read too much. Study well within the syllabus and the relevant books only. Don't go outside the syllabus.

There is no end to the reading material and the books. Our preparation time is limited and we cannot afford to read everything we feel important. Having books is good. Spending on them is never a waste. But this exam requires focus and good quality reading material. *Give your precious time to the topics mentioned in the syllabus only. Don't go out of it and try to cover the unnecessary topics.* You will not only lose time but also your focus, energy and momentum. This will clutter your study room and table. If there are only a few pages which are important in a book, read only them. Get them Xeroxed or make notes and then leave the book. Small thing, but neglected by many.

Having more books is also bad because you will not be able to read and revise all of them. And you will feel bad that you have not read all the books you have. In fact at the far end of preparation you should be dealing only with your notes and answers written by you.

Part III
Mistakes of Exam Strategies

CHAPTER 1

Warmup

"If you spend too much time warming up,
you'll miss the race. If you don't warm up at all,
you may not finish the race."

– Grand Heidrich

In every exam we find the initial time as the most difficult time. Our body and especially our mind require an initial warm up to make it fluent and ready for the exam. So that we can think faster and the answers come faster in our mind.

You can do simple stretching exercises, before the exam, for some time to increase blood supply to brain. Simple long breathing will improve the oxygen level of body. This will activate your mind. Stress and anxiety of exam will thus go down. Remember you may not be able to remove the stress and anxiety without doing anything. It is going to be there. You can only manage and control it.

Learn and study about the mind gym. Study a few books on memory and mind. Lot of research is being going on brain. Find out your own relaxing and warm up technique. Practice it and live with it. Those of you who play sports know the importance of warm up.

One simple technique before the start of the exam is to think about an important topic from the syllabus. Start making a few notes on that topic recalling from your memory and brainstorming. You can do this for 5-10 minutes. Another is alternate nostril breathing for a few minutes.

Arrive early at the exam location. Check and re-check the location and time of the exam. The idea is to make you comfortable before the start of the exam.

CHAPTER 2

Know the Whole

"If you know the enemy and
know yourself, your victory
will not stand in doubt"

– Sun Tzu, The Art of War

Not reading the entire question paper before you start answering the questions is one common and easily correctable mistake. There are many essential decisions to be taken based on this at the start of the exam.

This is required to get a feel of the question paper at the start of the exam. It is essential to know your sequence of answering the question. It is of great consequence to know how many questions you are going to attempt and how many questions you will be leaving. It is vital in deciding questions to be attempted where there is a choice. It is paramount in deciding how much time we are going to give to each mark (explained in next chapter). You will not miss any important instructions.

The surprises are eliminated at the start itself. You mind start working subconsciously on all the questions. You can mark the questions where you have no idea about the answer and must not waste time. Attempting such questions will reduce our strike rate.

So, if at the start of a cross country race you know the track, the potholes, the shortcuts, and the uphill and downhill slopes you can run faster and finish better.

CHAPTER 3
Get Busy Writing

"It is quality rather than quantity that matters."

– Seneca

There is a prescribed word limit for every question. This is the expectation of the examiner from you. No examiner is going to count the exact number of words you have written and grade you according to that.

So while we write the answers we get engaged in the number of words. We bother unnecessarily about them. We start counting them. We start counting lines and pages. Every question has prescribed maximum marks. Devote time as per the maximum marks and forget about the word limit. The entire exam is limited by time and not by the words. Cultivate the habit of fast reading, thinking and writing. This is all we need and it will come by practice. *The only difference between an "aspirant having extraordinary chance" to succeed and "one with no chance" is practice.*

The habit of bothering about word limit is bad because of many reasons. The word limit will give you no idea of the time that can be devoted on that particular question. Time management for the exam will thus suffer and you will not be able to give your best shot. You will miss some question this way even though you could have answered them. You will in some way try to estimate the number of words that you have written and more to be written in the answer while writing one. This could be by counting lines or pages that you have written. This is an absolutely unwarranted and waste of time. Even if we do not have anything good to write you will tend to repeat what you wrote already for the sake of fulfilling the word limit. Ultimately it is only a distraction.

You will ask now "How do we decide then how much to write?" Well, the correct question to ask at this stage is "How do we decide then how much time to devote to an answer?" I will explain it though an example. Assume that the question paper is of 300 marks and you have 3 hours to answer. Apart from writing the answer you need time for –

1. Reading the entire question paper at the start of the exam.

2. Reading and understanding the individual question before you start answering it.

3. Time for making rough draft and thinking before writing an essay type answer.

4. At the end of answering all questions you need time to check if you have mentioned all question numbers correctly in your answer sheet(this can be saved though practice).

5. Miscellaneous time required—drinking water, asking for supplementary answer sheets, tagging the sheets with main answer sheet, going to washroom (Some of these can again be eliminated with practice).

So time available for answer writing is:

180 minutes – time required for (1+2+3+4+5)

A reasonable estimate of (1+2+3+4+5) is around 30 minutes.

Therefore time left for answer writing = 150 minutes.

If I assume that you will attempt the full exam (with practice you will reach close to this level), the time available for answering 1 mark question is

150/300 = 0.5 minutes per mark

= 30 seconds per mark

Therefore for an N mark question you need to devote N/2 minutes. A 2 marks question may be devoted 1 minute. A 10 marks question 5 minutes. 20 marks question 10 minutes. Just divide the marks by 2 and you will have reasonable estimate of writing time of that question.

Now, how do you manage this in exam? Practice it during mock tests. Get used to a digital watch with a big display. Once you are used to taking exams in this manner it will come naturally to you. And before writing you will get to know about time required for a particular question.

You can get out of this habit no matter how long you are into it. It is never too late. Practice my dear friend. Practice will give the power.

So, get busy writing and not get busy counting.

Chapter 4
Sequence of Answers

"A sequence works in a
way a collection never can."

– George Murray

Every exam has a lot of question to be answered. Sequence of answers is the sequence in which you decide to answer the questions. For prelims, there is no convincing reason to change the sequence of answering from that of exam.

For the mains, the sequence has to be decided as not all questions are of same weightage. There are questions with big and small stakes. Your level of comfort in answering them is different. While in some you can do very well, you may not be aware of a few answers. Also, unlike prelims the answer sheet is going to be evaluated by an examiner.

It is better to write a long answer question first followed by short answer questions. Reason is that answering a long answer first sets the flow. More effort, in terms of thinking and writing, is required to answer long answer question. This builds the momentum for rest of the paper. It is better to deal the short answer questions when your momentum is high. Even if you miss a few short answer questions it doesn't matter much.

Also, leave the question you do not know at all or poorly for the end. This is what I experienced. It worked well for me.

You could very well have a counter view or doing it in the traditional way from first to last. Whatever be the sequence, have a thoughtful decision about it. Practice your preferred sequence during the mock tests. Have a preference for one of the sequence and have your reasons about it. It is too important to be left for the D day.

CHAPTER 5
Know the Question

"understanding a question is half an answer."
– Socrates

Not understanding the question is one common mistake. The mistake is so unknowingly done that we are never able to discover it. We must read the question and think for a moment what the examiner wants. If it is not clear, better re-read it.

There is an overwhelming tendency to write about what we have studied during our preparation on that particular topic of question. We forget about the requirement of the question. Our brain gets into the business of recalling whatever we have studied about that topic and we start writing based on our recollection. Generally the questions are very specific and we need to limit ourselves to the question itself. From the first line start writing the answer and keep on writing about it. Stay away from beating around the bush and touching the actual question in a few lines only.

If you do not know the topic well don't try to put unnecessary things for the sake of fulfilling the world limit. The examiners are smart. They will catch you on this. It is wastage of time to write unnecessary things for the sake of word limit. Instead of this, devote time for answering other questions. Sometimes we start guessing the answer and start writing.

The answer to essay type question is both about your knowledge and presentation. It needs to have a structure in terms of introduction, main body and conclusion. Use sentences rather than bullet points.

There are certain command words in question through which the examiner assesses. Here is a list of the command words and what is generally expected by the examiner.

Compare	means you should give the similarities and the differences between two things.
Contrast	means you need to only list the differences between two things. Outline is to give the main points, It's the same as "explain briefly". Draw "the big picture". Give an overview of the main factors or the most important ideas.
Explain	means you need to give a fuller, longer answer with several points. Answer the question "How?". What is the principle? You may also need to answer the question "why?" and/or "where?" and "when?" as part of your description of "how?".
Describe	means give a fuller, longer answer. What is it? How does it work? Within the time limit available give a detailed account of the subject. More simply—'Write down...' Tell

	the examiner in your own words what/ how/ or why something happens.
Illustrate	give the illustrated account or with the aid of diagrams/graphs/maps. Show what something is like. Give some clear examples.
Evaluate	involves judgment and opinion. When we evaluate we will make some comment about how important, significant or valuable something is. How valid is it? How good is it? How well does something work? Come to a conclusion after analyzing the evidence. How good or bad/successful or unsuccessful something is. This is an opinion based response but it may require you to provide evidence for your points and clear explanations as to why you think the way you do.
Analyse	consider something carefully and in detail in order to understand or explain it. Look closely at the detail; give reasons why or how something is done and the effect of this.
Argue	persuade by showing evidence that something is true, or the course of action which should be taken. Give reasons why something should or should not be done. Put forward a point of view in a structured and reasoned way. Usually one sided but takes account of other points of view.

Comment on	Don't just describe it. Offer your own opinion on the issue. You could offer other opinions and compare them. This requires you to analyze and evaluate in a balanced way with reasons.
Criticize	make decisions. Analyze and make a judgment. Referring to the opinions of other people (particularly acknowledged experts) is useful when supporting your judgment. When offering criticism, always try to include constructive suggestions as to how any problems could be overcome.
Define	give a very short answer to the question "What is it?" Give a precise statement to provide a short, unambiguous explanation of the meaning of a concept or term. A definition should only contain essential information.
Discuss	debate advantages and disadvantages. List pros and cons. Argue the merits of different points of view about something. Don't just explain or describe. Also known as 'examine' and 'consider'. Give the main reasons 'for' and 'against' and come to a conclusion.
Justify	give solid evidence for. Go on to a conclusion and support it with facts and figures. Maybe also give evidence against opposite interpretations.
Prove	show that.... Support with facts, figures, evidence, or examples.

Relate	tell the "story" of how things are connected. How they affect each other.
Review	make a survey of, examining the subject in a critical way.
State	put it "in a nutshell". Present in a short, clear sentence or two. This could be followed by justification if the question requires support of your statement.
Summarize	give a short account of the main conclusions or ideas. Don't introduce any new ideas.
To what extent	how far? Up to what point? It's usually best not to be 100% in agreement or disagreement, nor to be in the middle: show you're aware of different, opposing opinions, but come down clearly on one side in your argument.
Trace	"How did it come about?" Give a short description of the order in which events happened. Comment on the causes and effects.
Examine	look closely at something and discuss in a balanced and detached way in order to come to a decision/ conclusion.
List	require single words or phrases. Sometimes the order will be important. Questions with this word in do not require any reasoning or explanation. Simply select the information required and write it.

Support you answer with evidences. Support your opinion with factual and logical evidences and avoid your personal opinion. You can give examples and quotes of famous authors on that topic to authenticate your reply.

There is a difference between answer writing for optional subject and General Studies. In General Studies do not make your answer complex by putting difficult concepts in it. *Keep it simple so that examiner can understand it. You can showcase your knowledge in you optional as you want as the examiner will be of the same field.*

CHAPTER 6

Don't Bother about Easy and Average

"Little things console us because little things afflict us."

– Blaise Pascal

Do you feel the urge to answer a question in a great detail when you know it very well? Do you think you can exploit the topic, you are comfortable with, by writing and explaining more? Do you think you can score very well in few question and ignore a few?

Well, the importance of the question is decided by the marks allotted to that question and not by your comfort level. It is not possible to compensate one answer by the other. Even by writing very well you will not be able to score well in a particular question at the cost of others. So, devote time to the answers based on the marks allotted to them rather than your knowledge.

There may be certain straight forward questions where you tend to write more crossing the time limit. Certain questions are slightly twisted and require more thinking. Such questions generally appear difficult. You tend to avoid or spend less time on them. *Well, the twisted and the tough questions are the one which differentiate the ordinary from the extraordinary.* The scope of scoring more than other candidates is high in the difficult questions.

I take an example. Suppose the exam has 10 questions to be answered. Six are based directly on the topics mentioned in the syllabus and belong to difficulty level from easy to average. Another four are twisted and require more insight, thinking and effort in answering and they belong to difficulty level from difficult to very difficult. In such a situation we make the mistake of concentrating on the easy questions more than the difficult. We give more time to the easy and average difficulty level question. You must realize that most of the aspirants will be able to answer these questions. They are not going to put you at top in terms of score. It is your score in the difficult question which will separate you from the rest.

CHAPTER 7
Tracking Time

"Time is what we want most,
but... what we use worst."

– William Penn

Why is it difficult for us to complete the entire question paper? Why are we forced to leave certain questions unanswered even though we know the answer? Why the real challenge is not to answer the question but to write the answer within a time limit? How thinking in terms of word limit for answer distracts us to keep track of time? How much time do we need to invest for a question?

The answer to these questions lies in utilization of time during exam. There is a prescribed word limit for every question. The number of words that you can write depends upon speed of your thinking and writing. You can write more number of words in the same time if your speed is fast. So the limiting factor is time and not the words. Time to be devoted to each question, in turn, then depends upon the marks allotted for that particular question.

You can calculate the time available per mark. It is total time available for writing answers divided by total marks.

Multiply this figure with marks and you will get the time available for a question. The time available with us for answering a 10 marks question is therefore half of that available for a 20 marks question. So keep on answering the question till your time is over on that question and forget about the word limit. The usual temptation is to cross the time limit for answering a question so as to make the answer more impressive. This will cascade into time deficit with every question. And in the end many questions will be compromised. *The best answer is not what we can write but what we can write in a time limit.*

You can keep track of time using a digital watch during exam. Get used to this through a lot of practice of mock tests. Sticking to the time limit for each question is the key to answering all questions.

So don't fall for the temptation of solving the easy questions only. Face the difficult also. You may require more time to think than to write in easy questions, but the reward will be more.

CHAPTER 8
Critical Thinking

"If we are not prepared to think for ourselves, and to make the effort to learn how to do this well, we will always be in danger of becoming slaves to the ideas and values of others due to our own ignorance."

– William Hughes

There is tendency amongst many aspirants to reproduce what they studied during preparation in their answers. Though the questions might be asking about something very specific from a topic, they tend to write general things they studied about the topic.

There are many reasons for this habit. First is poor understanding of the question. Then there is this godforsaken habit of cramming and memorizing. The aspirants who have not done enough of answer writing practice also fall for this style. Poor management of time and inability to think also forces to take this shortcut approach. Inadequate mock test practice will further aggravate it. And most important is lack of confidence in oneself to write after thinking and understanding in one's own words.

This practice will further give you a false feeling of doing well in the exam. After an unsuccessful attempt this weakness will be difficult to diagnose. So take your time. Understand the question. Practice a lot of writing and mock tests. Earn your confidence. Think critically about the question and then answer. Hit at the target in one shot.

CHAPTER 9
Introduction and Conclusion

"God always shows us the introduction and the conclusion of our dreams to excite us about the whole task. He doesn't want to show us the daunting body of our dreams because He knows that we'll rather run away from our dreams than to pursue them."

– Euginia Herlihy

Not writing introduction and conclusion in essay type questions is a serious omission. Every essay type question at the very outset requires introduction about the answer we are writing. It also needs a final paragraph summarizing what has been said in the main body of the answer with you deductions and comments.

A fine introduction gives the examiner a good initial impression. The introduction arouses the interest of the examiner and indicates why the topic is of interest in the first place. This paragraph gives the examiner an idea of the arguments being made or considered and the reasons why the issue is important. The introduction must be such as which define the importance and relevance of the question.

Try to imagine for some time that the topic asked is, the most, important topic to think and write about. It could be approximately 10-15% of the length of your answer.

The body of the essay is where your discussion takes place. It contains issues to support your main argument. The argument is structured in a linear way: each issue is presented with supporting evidence. It is around 70-80% of your answer.

Conclusion is the last paragraph (approximately 10-15% of the length of the essay). It contains a summary of the main points. Statement about your main argument and comments on the topic based on the information provided by you in the main body. It should not contain any new information. It should simply be a reiteration of your main points or arguments.

CHAPTER 10

Why Question the Question?

"It is not that I'm so smart.
But I stay with the questions much longer."

– Albert Einstein

There is no less deserving or more deserving question in the exam. Topics of syllabus could be less important or more important based on their frequency in the previous year's exams. Once it has been asked and prescribed some marks it is important and deserves your 100%. Its real world importance has no value for us.

In many of the question we might feel that topic asked is not that important. But don't convey it to the examiner. Let it be known to the examiner that every question is important to you. The question must be justified as the most important topic though your introduction. It is only when we realize the importance of a particular topic; we are able to think big about that topic. The quality of answer improves. This way you will not be questioning the question itself in your answer. You will not be contradicting it.

So, from now on every question is a great question. A big question. Think that it is the ultimate topic in the universe. You will come up with much better answer.

No doubt, this mistake is easy to discover and correct.

CHAPTER 11

Big Isn't Better

"Vigorous writing is concise. A sentence should contain no unnecessary words, a paragraph no unnecessary sentences, for the same reason that a drawing should have no unnecessary lines and a machine no unnecessary parts. This requires not that the writer make all his sentences short, or that he avoid all detail and treat his subjects only in outline, but that every word tell."

– William Strunk Jr., The Elements of Style

When we are short of words we tend to fill the answer with unnecessary facts and details. This mistake is direct consequence of giving unnecessary importance to the word limit rather than time limit for answering a question. While doing so we are not answering the question but wavering around it.

This is a total waste of time. You are not going to be assessed based on the size of the answer. If you don't have enough words you can borrow words of established thinkers on that topic. You may draw diagram or map explaining your answer. You can take examples from real life to substantiate your answer. You can think about it in the exam itself and write it down. *Some questions are best answered by trusting your brain power and thinking about them even though you might not have read about them during your preparation.*

Don't expect every question to be straight forward from the syllabus. Don't just try to recall what you have read and prepared. Have confidence in yourself. You have prepared well and practiced enough and you can write well about it. Think in terms of competition. Think of answering an awkward question better than others.

In other words, get down focusing in your answers and writing what is relevant. Think real time and trust the reasoning ability of your brain. And don't just emit what you read. Avoid the unnecessary as nobody is going to give score for that.

CHAPTER 12

Care for Contradictions

"Read not to contradict and confute,
nor to believe and take for granted
...but to weigh and consider."

– Francis Bacon

Our answers must be free from contradictions. This is a common mistake. Sometime we contradict ourselves in the same question. And sometimes we contradict ourselves in the same exam in two different answers if not in the same answer. It is like having two conflicting view on the same issue. Or two conflicting bent of mind.

We do it unintentionally most of the times. This is because of poor understanding of the fundamentals or lack of concentration during the exam. Either way, we shall be penalized for this mistake. *And while we calculate our chances after the exam is over we tend to overestimate our score.*

This is difficult to identify whether we have done it in exam or not. The mistake can be corrected easily by taking a lot of mock test and getting them graded through your coaches.

CHAPTER 13
Handwriting

"A bad handwriting is as annoying to a reader ... as an irritating voice is to a listener."

– Mokokoma Mokhonoana

The exam demands fast handwriting to answer all the questions. You would not like to leave a question unanswered because of paucity of time, when you know the answer well. You may study and prepare well for the exam but if you are finally constrained to write, all that was needed to be written, you will be disappointed. Therefore we need to develop the skill of fast handwriting during our preparation to do well.

We also need to develop neat handwriting if not a good handwriting. We may not be able to change our handwriting but at least we can make it neat. This will improve our presentation. *You can have better handwriting by changing space between letters, words, sentences and line spacing.* And believe me when you start working consciously, it will improve. Your answer writing and mock test practice will help you to improve.

Many a times there is a tendency to write bigger fonts. This may be part of your natural handwriting. Some might think in terms of making their answer look bigger and cover more number of pages in the answer sheet. This is not advisable because writing bigger fonts will reduce your speed of writing. Bigger fonts require more number of pages to answer. More number of pages means you will lose track of what you have written on the previous pages on the same answer. You tend to lose coherence in our answer. It is difficult for the examiner also. The requirement of supplementary answer sheets also arises. Supplementary answer sheet is again an avoidable hassle.

So, have a good pen to write fast and practice with it. Choose a pen type and use it all through your preparation and the exams. The same type of pen for everything you write. A pen for an aspirant is like a gun for a soldier. And no soldier likes to change or leave his particular gun. He practices it with it at the firing range and uses the same for the battlefield. Let your pen be one of your body parts. Never depart from it.

Chapter 14

Sleep Well Before Exam

"Sleep is the best meditation."

– Dalai Lama

The exam is very demanding and it puts you in lot of pressure and intimidation. Pressure and intimidation cannot be eradicated. But it can be managed by practicing your mind. Take so many practice exams so that you do not feel the final exam special. Getting this awe of examination out of mind is necessary. It is only this way that we can sleep well when it is most required i.e. night before the examination.

Don't try to cover the entire syllabus through revision before the exam. Give your mind sometime before the exam to relax. Poor sleep has also one more reason. It is when we do not set our biological clock. The duration and timing of study and sleep sets a biological clock, if repeated over a few days. Have a sleep and study cycle which matches with the exam timings. A biological clock set by studying during the night time in late hours and sleeping during the day will not allow you to sleep well when it is most required.

So set your biological clock in such a manner to match your performance peak with the exam timing.

Conclusion

Most of the reasons mentioned above are fatal to your selection. The exam takes your one full year. If not fatal they will certainly reduces your chances of selections. These are the handicaps. All of them are matters of attitude and habit. Some of them are known. Some are not known even after exhausting all the attempts. The mere idea of them will allow your brain to work on them. You can save years of hard work and money.

Of course there are some trivial reasons for failure. I have not discussed them and assumed that you must have known them. Some of the mistakes are committed so unknowingly that we don't even know if we committed them or not. So after the exam, when we calculate, our expected score will be on higher side. This will only reveal to us when we know the result and our score. Even at that stage we shall not be able to identify the mistake.

The only difference between an "aspirant having extraordinary chance" to succeed and "one with no chance" is practice. It is only through practice that you identify your mistakes you commit while taking the examination. That's why the focus of this book is to make aspirants realize that studying and knowledge is only a necessary condition but not sufficient condition for the exam. The sufficient